D0407387

LIBERTY
OR DEATH

A Creative Minds Biography

LIBERTY OR DEATH

A Story about Patrick Henry

by Stephanie Sammartino McPherson

illustrations by Nicolas Debon

Carolrhoda Books, Inc./Minneapolis

For my parents, Angelo and Marion Sammartino

This book is available in two editions:
Library binding by Carolrhoda Books, Inc.,
a division of Lerner Publishing Group
Soft cover by First Avenue Editions,
an imprint of Lerner Publishing Group
241 First Avenue North
Minneapolis, MN 55401 U.S.A.

Website address: www.lernerbooks.com

Library of Congress Cataloging-in-Publication Data

McPherson, Stephanie Sammartino.
    Liberty or death : a story about Patrick Henry / by Stephanie
Sammartino McPherson ; illustrated by Nicolas Debon.
        p.   cm. — (A creative minds biography)
    Includes bibliographical references and index.
    Summary: A biography of the Virginia lawyer, politician, and patriot
whose great powers of speech helped inspire colonists to support the cause
of American liberty at the start of the Revolutionary War.
    ISBN: 1-57505-178-8 (lib. bdg. : alk. paper)
    ISBN: 0-87614-930-1 (pbk. : alk. paper)
    1. Henry, Patrick, 1736-1799—Juvenile literature. 2. Legislators—
United States—Biography—Juvenile literature. 3. United States.
Continental Congress—Biography—Juvenile literature. 4. United States—
Politics and government—1775-1783—Juvenile literature. 5. Virginia—
Politics and government—1775-1783—Juvenile literature. [1. Henry,
Patrick, 1736-1799. 2. Legislators. 3. United States—Politics and
government—1775-1783.] I. Debon, Nicolas, ill. II. Title. III. Series.
E302.6.H5 M39 2002
973.3'092—dc21   2001006471

Manufactured in the United States of America
1 2 3 4 5 6 – JR – 08 07 06 05 04 03

Table of Contents

1

Backwoods Boyhood

Patrick Henry lay on his back by the creek and dangled a fishing line into the water. Sometimes hours would pass before he felt the tug of a fish, but Patrick was patient. He loved being alone in the Virginia woods with nothing to do but relax and try to recognize bird calls. If he only listened long and hard enough, maybe he could figure out what the birds were saying.

Even when Patrick did have something else to do— like study his lessons—he sometimes snuck away to the forest. It wasn't that he disliked learning. Patrick was a bright boy. But on certain fine days, the lure of the sunshine and the towering trees was too strong for him to resist. Tomorrow seemed a long way off. Patrick would rather enjoy a day of freedom and talk his way out of trouble later.

Born May 29, 1736, Patrick lived with his parents at Studley Plantation. The Henrys's small farm was surrounded by locust trees and overlooked the nearby Pamunkey River. Patrick's father, originally from Scotland, had settled in the British colony of Virginia and married a beautiful, wealthy widow. Patrick had an older brother, William, and seven little sisters. He also had a half brother, John Syme, from his mother's first marriage. Studley had belonged to John Syme's father. John would inherit the land when he became an adult.

Patrick's father was ambitious and well respected. Besides running the plantation, he became a court judge and helped manage his local church. But despite his hard work, he was not a talented farmer. The family had enough to eat and decent clothes to wear but little else. John Henry certainly didn't have the money to send his sons to college. He had been to college himself, however. He taught his sons subjects they didn't learn in the small, local school.

Patrick did well at the Latin, Greek, and ancient history his father taught him. He especially liked mathematics. But he would still much rather roam the countryside than read or study. Hanover County had creeks, deep woods, and teeming wildlife. Sometimes friends joined Patrick canoeing on the South Anna

River. Patrick liked to suggest they all go swimming. Then, while everyone was still deciding, Patrick would whip off his clothes, stand up, and dive into the water, upsetting the boat. Seconds later he'd appear again, grinning at his friends who had fallen into the river in their shirts and breeches.

Whether in water or on land, Patrick liked to show off a bit. He picked the tallest trees to climb. Sometimes he also swung from low branches, flinging himself across the creek. In fact, Patrick was so daring that he once broke his collarbone. It was hard to stay indoors during his long recovery period. One day, with nothing better to do, Patrick picked up a flute. Over the next few weeks and months he taught himself to play popular tunes. He could also scrape out lively tunes on the fiddle.

As he grew older, Patrick's musical talents must have made him popular at social gatherings. He was a cheerful, friendly boy. Patrick liked people and had a knack for telling stories, but he was often quiet when neighbors came to visit. He hardly seemed to glance at the guests at all. Shaking their heads, people thought he was simply lost in a world of his own. But once the family was alone again, Patrick could recall everything that was said, from talk of Indian raids along the Virginia borders to the spring tobacco planting to the last Sunday's sermon. Patrick hadn't really been daydreaming. He was listening very carefully and trying to understand people.

Patrick listened especially hard when he went to the Reverend Samuel Davies's church. Sarah Henry often took Patrick and his sisters to hear the reverend's sermons. Spellbound, Patrick listened to the minister's voice rise and fall. Like a clever lawyer building his case, the Reverend Davies breathed feeling into every word. He knew when to pause, when to whisper, when to thunder. It wasn't just what the reverend said that inspired his listeners, Patrick realized. It was how he said it.

After the services, Patrick would hitch the horse back to the carriage and take his mother and sisters home. Sarah Henry wanted to know what her son thought of the sermons. As they drove along, she often asked Patrick to restate what had been said. Patrick threw himself wholeheartedly into the telling. He didn't just repeat the minister's main points. He imitated the Reverend Davies's powerful speaking style. Convincing an audience—even if it was only his mother and sisters—came naturally to Patrick.

When Patrick's half brother, John Syme, reached adulthood, he inherited Studley Plantation. Now that Patrick's father no longer managed the plantation

for his stepson, Patrick's family was forced to move.

They packed up their belongings and traveled through twenty miles of dense forest to arrive at their new home. Patrick's father named it Mount Brilliant, though it never quite lived up to its name. The house was not as big as Studley, and the plantation was even less successful.

John Henry was worried about his sons' futures. He had seven daughters who needed dowries, money, or land to take when they married to help them start new lives. How could he possibly provide for Patrick and William too? Finally he came up with a plan. First he sent fifteen-year-old Patrick and his sixteen-year-old brother to work for some Scottish merchants. That way they would learn about how to run a successful business. After about one year, John Henry bought a supply of household goods such as locks, shoes, fabrics, and pocketknives. Then he set the boys up in business near their old home of Studley. They would live with their half brother, John Syme, while they sold their wares.

The problem was that Patrick and William weren't all that interested in running a store. Patrick had never spent very much time reading, but he suddenly decided he would much rather read than wait on customers. Farmers often entered the shop to find

Patrick lost in the pages of *Robinson Crusoe* or *Don Quixote.* If he was in the middle of an exciting part, Patrick might not even bother to look up.

When he wasn't reading, he often entertained people with exciting stories. And he told customers who couldn't afford his wares not to worry. They should just take what they needed and pay when they could. Unfortunately, some people couldn't afford to pay at all. Without money, the Henry brothers couldn't buy new stock. They struggled to keep their store afloat.

But there was a good side to Patrick's situation. Living in his old neighborhood, he got to renew his friendship with pretty Sarah (Sallie) Shelton, the innkeeper's daughter. Patrick had probably known Sallie since they were both small children, but he began to see her in a new way. He looked forward to meeting her at the barbecues and country dances that livened up the neighborhood. Sallie found Patrick's friendliness and sense of humor appealing.

But no amount of friendliness could save the store. Patrick and William realized they weren't earning enough money with their business. After only about a year, they went bankrupt.

2

Country Lawyer

Without his store, Patrick had no way to make a living. It didn't seem like a wise time to be thinking about marriage. But Patrick was determined to make Sallie his wife. First, however, he had to convince his parents—and Sallie's—that he was ready for such a big step.

Whether it was his enthusiasm, his well-chosen words, or simply his obvious love for Sallie, Patrick got both sets of parents to agree to the wedding. That fall, in 1754, eighteen-year-old Patrick married sixteen-year-old Sallie. Family and friends surrounded the young couple, as Patrick's uncle, a minister, performed the service in the front parlor of the bride's home.

Soon Patrick and Sallie were setting up housekeeping

on a small farm named Pine Slash. Sallie's father had given the land and small wooden house as part of his daughter's dowry. He also gave Patrick six slaves to help turn the sandy soil into profitable tobacco fields.

Walking across his land studded with scrub pine, Patrick scarcely knew what to do. He had never been a farmer before and had to learn how to care for his crops. With the help of his slaves, Patrick mixed tobacco seeds with ashes, planted them carefully, and covered them with branches and leaves. After the seeds sprouted and grew, Patrick had to transplant them into carefully prepared fields. He spent months weeding, trimming leaves, and crushing fat caterpillars that ate the tobacco leaves.

Soon Patrick had another reason to work extra hard. In the summer of 1755, Sallie gave birth to a little girl named Martha, nicknamed Patsy. At nineteen, Patrick was young to be a father. But family responsibilities were making him grow up fast. He worked constantly to provide a comfortable household for his wife and daughter. By early fall, Patrick and his men were picking the tobacco and setting the large leaves out to dry in his shed.

After so much hard work, Patrick had hoped for a larger harvest. Little rain had fallen that summer, and frosts had come early. Much of the crop was ruined.

16

Even the tobacco Patrick did have was hard to sell. The French and Indian War was to blame. This raging war between the French and the British on colonial soil had made travel through the western wilderness dangerous. Business had almost come to a standstill.

Throughout the next year, Patrick continued to work in the fields all day and enjoy his family at night. As Patsy grew into a lively toddler, Patrick could entertain her with his fiddle or with bird calls. On fine afternoons, he might snatch a few moments to carry her through the woods, sharing the sights and sounds he loved so much.

In the spring of 1757, Patsy's little brother John was born. Just when Patrick needed to work harder than ever to support his family, a fire broke out in the Pine Slash farmhouse. No one was hurt, but the house was in ruins. There were few belongings left to carry to the nearby cabin where the family was forced to live. Patrick and Sallie hoped they would not stay long in the cramped, uncomfortable rooms. With a successful tobacco crop, maybe they could afford to build something better.

But rain was still scarce, and Patrick had another bad harvest. The family felt ready to burst out of their meager cabin. Finally Sallie's father suggested that the Henrys move into his inn across from the Hanover

Court House, about half a mile from Pine Slash. Although Patrick continued to farm his land and even opened another small store, he also helped his father-in-law run the tavern at the inn. Always friendly despite his misfortunes, Patrick played his violin in the crowded dining hall. Often barefoot, he mingled happily with the guests, exchanging news and jokes as he served them drinks.

Many discussions at the tavern centered on the court cases being tried across the street. Lawyers and clients relived the trials in vivid detail. Patrick could not get enough of such talk. He wanted to know much more than anyone could remember. So Patrick began attending the monthly court sessions, too.

Squeezed onto a wooden bench with the other spectators, he listened to the lawyers argue back and forth. Patrick thought that he could argue just as convincingly. He thought it would be exciting to speak in a courtroom. And he could make more money to support his family. This was especially important because the farm and store were still doing poorly.

Patrick didn't expect much help in meeting his goal. There were no law schools in the colonies. A few men went to Great Britain to get their legal training. Others worked with an established lawyer for several years before they learned enough to pass the exam needed to become a lawyer. Patrick was certainly not going to wait for several years before he started practicing law. Somehow he would quickly learn everything he needed to pass the test on his own.

Patrick continued to attend court sessions and listen eagerly to legal talk in the tavern. He borrowed some law books and studied late into the night. It was skimpy preparation. But Patrick didn't waste time worrying about what he didn't know. He knew that he was clever and that words came quickly to him. Picturing his future, Patrick was certain he could hold his own in a courtroom. After only several months, he felt ready to prove himself.

In April of 1760, Patrick set off for Williamsburg, Virginia, to take his law test. The fifty-mile trip was the longest he had ever taken. He had to coax his horse through puddles, mud, and streams swollen by spring rains. But Patrick was too impatient to wait for the roads to dry out. The day after his arrival in Williamsburg, he walked across the wide lawn of the Governor's Palace to the home of his first examiner. One by one, Patrick would meet with four established lawyers. He would need the signatures of at least two of them on his license in order to plead cases in court.

One examiner, John Randolph, was so shocked by Patrick's ragged clothes and informal manners that he told him to simply go away. Such an awkward young man could never become a lawyer. But Patrick wouldn't take no for an answer. Finally, Randolph agreed to ask him a few questions. Then he asked him a few more—and a few more. The exam went on for several hours while Randolph marveled at Patrick's sharp mind and vivid way of speaking. Patrick didn't know nearly enough about legal rules, but he knew how to express his views clearly.

Then Randolph pretended to disagree with one of Patrick's replies. Patrick argued his point as thoroughly as if he were standing in a courtroom. Afterwards, Randolph took Patrick into his office, lined with law books. "You have never seen these books. . . ," declared Randolph, "yet you are right and I am wrong." Glancing once more at Patrick's rustic clothing he added with amusement, "I will never trust to appearances again." He signed Patrick's license and predicted he would be a fine lawyer.

Patrick had already received a signature from another judge. Now he was ready to practice law, and he could hardly wait to make Judge Randolph's prediction come true. Relying on friends and acquaintances, he spread the word that he was available to take cases. Soon he was riding to courthouses all over western Virginia as a lawyer for new clients.

Although he missed his family, Patrick made the most of his travels. Riding through the woods, he often stopped to hunt a squirrel or a few ducks. When he reached the courthouse in his soiled clothing with a string of small animals slung over his horse, he looked like a rugged frontiersman.

Once inside the building, however, Patrick became unmistakably a lawyer. Most of his cases had to do with small debts or questions of land ownership. None of them had any importance beyond the few people involved. But whenever Patrick addressed the court—whether he spoke about a stolen hog or illegally chopped trees—people listened. Patrick could make the most trivial subject fascinating.

While Patrick handled small cases, he also followed bigger ones. One important controversy concerned the Anglican Church, the official religion of the colony of Virginia. According to the law, Anglican ministers received their salary in tobacco. When crops were abundant, tobacco might sell for a low price. When the harvest was scarce, buyers were willing to pay more for tobacco. But the ministers always got the same amount of tobacco. As the price of tobacco went up and down, so did their salary. For several years now, crops had been poor. That made the price of tobacco skyrocket. Virginians did not think they could afford to pay the ministers the full amount of tobacco.

To solve the problem, the Virginia's lawmakers passed a law that allowed the ministers to be paid two pennies for every pound of tobacco they were due. The ministers felt cheated because tobacco was selling for much more than two cents per pound. They took their complaint all the way to Britain, where King George III struck down Virginia's so-called Two-Penny Law. Pleased by their success, some ministers decided to sue for the extra money.

In November 1763, the Hanover court sided with the Reverend James Maury against Thomas Johnson, a government official who paid the ministers. The minister deserved more money, declared the judge. The only question was how much.

To most observers it seemed that the trial, known as the Parson's case, was over. That's certainly what Mr. Johnson's lawyer thought when he turned the second part of the case over to his young friend Patrick Henry. All Patrick had to do was keep the sum given to the reverend as low as possible.

But Patrick saw the case in larger terms. Here was his chance to speak for the good of the entire colony. He would take a stand that people would never forget.

If This Be Treason

Many people had been surprised and disappointed by the outcome of the Parson's case. They thought the ministers should care more about the good of the people than about their salaries. After all, higher salaries for the ministers meant higher taxes for the people. Farmers, merchants, and country gentlemen as well as ministers turned out to see what the court would award the Reverend Maury.

Patrick had never spoken before such a large crowd. He was so anxious he even asked his uncle, an Anglican minister, to leave. It didn't help matters that the judge hearing the case was Patrick's own father.

onsisted of two parts: the Council and the House of Burgesses. The twelve Council members, or Counselors, were appointed by the king for life. The Burgesses were elected by male property owners in Virginia. Now that Patrick owned land in Louisa, he was qualified to become that county's representative, or Burgess. In May 1765, a special election was held. No one ran against Patrick for the empty seat in the House of Burgesses.

The General Assembly's spring session had already begun. As Patrick galloped towards Williamsburg, the capital city where the Assembly met, he wondered what the Burgesses would do about the latest political crisis. Since the earliest colonial settlements, colonists had been taxed only by their local Assemblies. Now the British Parliament wanted to create a new tax with its proposed Stamp Act. Parliament said the tax was needed to help pay for the French and Indian War, which had been fought on American soil.

Although the colonists had no representatives in Parliament, the British lawmakers would decide how the tax money was to be used. The colonial government would have no say at all. If Parliament passed the Stamp Act, the colonists would be taxed on almost all printed materials. People would have to pay for special stamps to place on everything from newspapers

He had a hard time beginning his argument before the judge and jury. Eyes downcast, the stoop-shouldered young lawyer mumbled nervously. No one in the room thought he could possibly make a difference in the case. Patrick's father looked ready to slide off his seat in embarrassment.

Then something happened. Patrick began to get excited—even angry—as he presented the people's side of the issue. He squared his shoulders, looked straight at his listeners, and began to speak in a powerful voice. With mounting passion, Patrick explained that the Two-Penny Law had been made for the good of the entire colony. No one—not even the king—had the right to strike it down as if it had never existed.

Listeners stared in wonder and admiration as Patrick continued his fiery speech. The king had a duty to accept all good laws passed by Parliament, Britain's lawmaking body, and colonial lawmakers. If he did not do this, he was guilty of "misrule." Patrick pressed his point to a bold conclusion. When the king acted like a tyrant, the people should stick with their law and ignore his commands.

"Treason!" gasped several shocked spectators. They thought Patrick wanted them to disobey the king. Their whispered accusation rippled through the room.

Patrick kept right on talking. Ministers should obey the law—not try to overthrow it, he said. In taking their complaint to Britain, the ministers had become enemies of Virginia. Even though the Reverend Maury had already won his court case, he should not be rewarded with a large sum of money.

It took the jury only a few minutes to agree with Patrick. They gave the Reverend Maury only a penny in back wages. Ministers exclaimed angrily, but small farmers and businessmen cheered the victory for self-government. Triumphantly the people lifted Patrick onto their shoulders and paraded him around the court-house square.

After the Parson's case, people began to take note of Patrick. Many new clients signed up for his legal services. As fees poured in, he began to plan a house on some land his father had given him in Louisa County. He and Sallie now had three children. The growing family was still living in the tavern across from the courthouse. Patrick could scarcely wait to build his own home. In the meantime, he decided to run for public office.

Like the other twelve British colonies, Virginia had its own self-governing body, or legislature, to make laws and raise taxes for the good of its citizens. Virginia's legislature was called the General Assembly.

He had a hard time beginning his argument before the judge and jury. Eyes downcast, the stoop-shouldered young lawyer mumbled nervously. No one in the room thought he could possibly make a difference in the case. Patrick's father looked ready to slide off his seat in embarrassment.

Then something happened. Patrick began to get excited—even angry—as he presented the people's side of the issue. He squared his shoulders, looked straight at his listeners, and began to speak in a powerful voice. With mounting passion, Patrick explained that the Two-Penny Law had been made for the good of the entire colony. No one—not even the king—had the right to strike it down as if it had never existed.

Listeners stared in wonder and admiration as Patrick continued his fiery speech. The king had a duty to accept all good laws passed by Parliament, Britain's lawmaking body, and colonial lawmakers. If he did not do this, he was guilty of "misrule." Patrick pressed his point to a bold conclusion. When the king acted like a tyrant, the people should stick with their law and ignore his commands.

"Treason!" gasped several shocked spectators. They thought Patrick wanted them to disobey the king. Their whispered accusation rippled through the room.

Patrick kept right on talking. Ministers should obey the law—not try to overthrow it, he said. In taking their complaint to Britain, the ministers had become enemies of Virginia. Even though the Reverend Maury had already won his court case, he should not be rewarded with a large sum of money.

It took the jury only a few minutes to agree with Patrick. They gave the Reverend Maury only a penny in back wages. Ministers exclaimed angrily, but small farmers and businessmen cheered the victory for self-government. Triumphantly the people lifted Patrick onto their shoulders and paraded him around the court-house square.

After the Parson's case, people began to take note of Patrick. Many new clients signed up for his legal services. As fees poured in, he began to plan a house on some land his father had given him in Louisa County. He and Sallie now had three children. The growing family was still living in the tavern across from the courthouse. Patrick could scarcely wait to build his own home. In the meantime, he decided to run for public office.

Like the other twelve British colonies, Virginia had its own self-governing body, or legislature, to make laws and raise taxes for the good of its citizens. Virginia's legislature was called the General Assembly.

It consisted of two parts: the Council and the House of Burgesses. The twelve Council members, or Counselors, were appointed by the king for life. The Burgesses were elected by male property owners in Virginia.

Now that Patrick owned land in Louisa, he was qualified to become that county's representative, or Burgess. In May 1765, a special election was held. No one ran against Patrick for the empty seat in the House of Burgesses.

The General Assembly's spring session had already begun. As Patrick galloped towards Williamsburg, the capital city where the Assembly met, he wondered what the Burgesses would do about the latest political crisis. Since the earliest colonial settlements, colonists had been taxed only by their local Assemblies. Now the British Parliament wanted to create a new tax with its proposed Stamp Act. Parliament said the tax was needed to help pay for the French and Indian War, which had been fought on American soil.

Although the colonists had no representatives in Parliament, the British lawmakers would decide how the tax money was to be used. The colonial government would have no say at all. If Parliament passed the Stamp Act, the colonists would be taxed on almost all printed materials. People would have to pay for special stamps to place on everything from newspapers